DEAD MAN WATCHING

THE INCREDIBLE STORY OF A MAN WHO WATCHED HIMSELF DIE AND LIVED TO TELL IT

DR. JOHN HAART

WESTBOW
PRESS®
A DIVISION OF THOMAS NELSON
& ZONDERVAN

Interior images by John Rolando

WestBow Press books may be ordered through booksellers or by contacting:

WestBow Press
A Division of Thomas Nelson & Zondervan
1663 Liberty Drive
Bloomington, IN 47403
www.westbowpress.com
1 (866) 928-1240

ISBN: 978-1-5127-8327-8 (sc)
ISBN: 978-1-5127-8328-5 (e)

Library of Congress Control Number: 2017905626

Print information available on the last page.

WestBow Press rev. date: 7/13/2017

For all of our dear family,
including seven adult children,
their spouses, and our twenty-two grandchildren,
in Canada and the United States.

The briefest possible compression of Paul's letter to the Hebrews about the meaning of faith is:

"Faith is being sure of what you hope for."

This book is about a lot of hope and faith. It has taken twenty years to produce this miraculous story, and it is the hope of the author that all those who venture here are prepared to meet the Author and Healer of all life.

"Jesus said to him, 'I will come and heal him.' But the centurion answered him. 'Lord, I am not worthy to have you come under my roof, but only say the word and my servant will be healed. For I am a man under authority, with soldiers under me; and I say to one, "Go," and he goes, and to another "Come," and he comes, and to my slave, "Do this," and he does it.' When Jesus heard him he marveled, and said to those who followed him, "Truly I say to you, not even in Israel have I found such faith….And to the centurion Jesus said, 'Go; be it done for you as you have believed.' And the servant was healed at that very moment" (Mathew 8.7-13).

ACKNOWLEDGMENTS

The author is indebted to many sources for assistance. First of all is my dear wife Erin, not only for her steadfast love and kindness over fifty years, but also for her great amount of help in the writing of this book. All the members of our family are also thanked for their prayer support over a lifetime of trials. Special thanks are given to our dear friend in Christ, David S., for his good counsel and support over many years. We are very grateful for Gayle M., and many others who have faithfully blessed us with their fervent prayers. Editing was of great help by Judy M., Denny and Margaret Ann W. "Without counsel plans go wrong, but with many advisers they succeed" (Proverbs 15:22). Many thanks are also given to staff at WestBow Press for their helpful guidance in the publication of *Dead Man Watching*.

And before all,

Thanks be to God!

PREFACE

This entire story is about the mercy of God. From beginning to multiple ends, it is a modern testimony of how God works in mysterious ways through and over many stages of a single life. The amazing revelation for all those who read my story is that I remain a man once dead, who is now writing and talking to you about the miraculous interventions of God in life and death. In a very real way this book is an *auto-obituary of a man who witnessed his own death and now lives to tell about it.*

A significant tandem benefit of reading this book is the medical advice that all of us should know. Some of these tips could actually save your life. In addition, there will be some relevant concerns about the impact on your health that often arises during times and seasons of sustained stress.

Do you know what will be the time and place of

your death? Of course not. This book was inspired to help you be prepared at any moment for that pivotal moment: "Pray for us sinners, now and at the hour of our death. Amen."

CONTENTS

THE BEGINNING OF THE END

by Erin

John Haart was born in 1945. He was raised Catholic, and eventually we married in 1966 in the Catholic Church. However, after a lifetime of Catholic schools and Mass, he was, as Evangelicals might claim, in need of salvation.

After a few years of marriage, we became aware of a new movement in the Catholic Church called the *Charismatic Renewal.* One Sunday evening, we found our way to a special talk by a well-known French-Canadian priest from Quebec. Our attendance was to be quite pivotal.

Sometime earlier we had gone on vacation to New York City and ended up in Greenwich Village at a Sunday flea market in a Jewish neighborhood. In the middle of a huge crowd, our attention was riveted on a red-headed girl in a brilliantly white shirt, standing slightly above the crowd. She was shouting phrases from the Bible as loudly as she could. John could just make out "For God so loved the world that He sent His only Son, that whoever believes in Him should not perish, but have eternal life" (John 3:16). Suddenly, an overripe tomato hit her with great velocity and created the image that she had been shot. Many more tomatoes followed, until she was actually blown off her soapbox in a shower of red. It was a real shock. The whole scene looked like an actual murder. The many familiar stories of saints and martyrs had previously made little impression on John. Here she was . . . suffering for her faith! He was brought to tears and could do nothing to help or reverse this very real-looking tragedy. An epiphany had happened, and for the first time in his adult life he was awakened to the suffering of Christ and the shed blood of the martyrs.

The unexpected response to the red-
headed girl's invitation.

The timing was set for us. Upon returning to our home that summer, we went to listen to the priest from Quebec for the first time. His two-hour sermon was the best we had ever heard, and as trained and practicing high school teachers, we were amazed that he held the capacity audience on the edge of their seats for the entire time. The conclusion included a call to come forward. We saw many in the crowd moving to the basement stairs in the front of the building for coffee and donuts . . . so we thought. However, much to our amazement when we arrived there, he was praying over each one, some of whom fell to the floor without injury. He was doing what is done for *Confirmation, Holy Orders and prayer for the sick (Extreme Unction)*, which includes the laying on of hands. Often in His ministry, Jesus healed the sick by reaching out and touching those who needed healing. Once, He healed a woman who secretly touched the hem of his garment, hoping to be healed. Jesus said, "Someone touched me; for I perceive that power has gone forth from me . . . And he said to her, "Daughter, your faith has made you well; go in peace" (Luke 8:46,48).

Following this second pivotal event, we started attending the *Life in the Spirit Seminars*. These meetings were held in small group settings. The lessons were basic evangelism, emphasizing the role and power of the Holy Spirit in a believer's life. The impact was substantial. John's logical mind was working against some of the message with the age-old criticism of Christianity: *If God is so good and merciful, why is there so much evil and suffering in the world?*

We had many heated discussions on the topic. He was ready to quit the sessions, but one night at the prayer meetings that were part of the seminars, another pivotal event took place. An announcement was made about a men's *Cursillo* (a short course in Christ) to take place the following weekend, an eight hour trip away. I spoke to one of the leaders and asked him to reach out to John with a personal invitation. Within minutes he was surrounded by a small group of the team. They gave him some details and insisted that he could and should call into work for a personal day in order to attend the *Cursillo*. The logistics to travel hundreds of miles for a weekend were impossible. But the next morning at 4:00 a.m., he was in a van bound for the monastery as one of twelve men, singing songs of praise.

The tightly packed course was a series of lectures and discussion groups leading to an opportunity for personal conversion. All was going very well until he found himself in need of some quiet time to process everything that was going on in his mind and spirit. He found the beautiful chapel of the monastery and thought he was all alone, privately praying in the front. After a long period of silence and questioning God, he snapped, called out for Jesus to forgive him, and began weeping uncontrollably for some time. When he finally was able to get up, he turned around and discovered a little nun in the last pew. She had quietly been there for the entire emotional breakdown. She simply smiled and blessed him as he left the chapel. Just as the red headed evangelist in New York remains an unidentified person with great impact on his life, so the little nun in the chapel is a blessed memory to this day.

He returned a changed man from the *Cursillo*. He had experienced a Pauline conversion, had been knocked off his intellectual horse, and would never be the same. I was amazed and could see the great change. He was full of joy . . . happy and loving. The following Monday he went back to high school teaching, wearing the substantial crucifix he was given at the conclusion of the *Cursillo*. It must have looked to faculty members and students like he had become a deacon or some other Christian minister.

Life went on with our four daughters and one

son: Marina, Melora, Monica, Michelle, and Mark. Later on, with the addition of more children (Marla and Micah), seven in all, we were a very happy and busy family. We were blessed with a tranquil and sometimes challenging life on a hobby farm twenty-five miles out of town. It was the Great White North, half way between east and west. His little joke was that he traveled from Eastern to Western Canada every day of the school year because the geographic center of the transcontinental highway was on his route.

PART 1

CHAPTER ONE

IN THE END

by John

This begins with the fact that what you are about to read in this book is real, did happen as reported, and was witnessed by doctors, nurses, and family members.

It all begins on a chilly afternoon on a hill in our northwestern town. We had rented our farm and moved into town to work in St. Anthony's, a Canadian and Italian parish. I was on my way home from another day of teaching at a local high school. Climbing up the steep hill with walls of snow on either side, I noticed an occasional, sharp pain in my chest, which eventually dissipated upon resting for a few minutes. After five separate stops, I made it through the front door of our home. *Very strange . . . What was that all about?*

I did not think too much more about it for that night; however, that all changed the next morning. (The statistical numbers on the most common time of heart attack is early morning.) I got out of bed with serious chest pains, sweating, nausea, and dry-heave vomiting. (*At that time I did not know it, but these are the classic signs of a heart attack.*) When I hit the floor at the top of the stairs outside my bedroom, our daughter Marla helped me up and insisted that we should drive to the closest hospital only two blocks away.

(*This is the point of serious caution about what to do next with a suspected heart attack.* **Never** *drive yourself or allow someone to take you. You need medical help immediately. CALL AN AMBULANCE . . . TO SAVE YOUR LIFE.*)

Of course, being in denial that anything was really wrong, I thought it was too much trouble. (*A couple of months previously, my EKG and stress test confirmed that I had no problems related to any heart or artery issues.*) After all, I was only fifty years old.

The piercing chest pains continued to increase without relenting, and when we reached the doorway of the Emergency Department, I stumbled through the electric doors and fell on the floor! Staff rushed to pick me up and put me on a gurney. Hospital alert codes were broadcast in the halls, and a group of medical staff gathered around the gurney. The cardiac signals on the heart monitor in the Emergency Room were very audible, and I was soon surrounded by three nurses and an ER doctor.

Under the intensely bright surgery lights, distressed voices were shouting orders in rapid succession. Soon there were more medical staff in the small room already crowded with medical apparatus, and the orders became quicker and louder. "More oxygen." etc. (*I later found that there were an increased number of people in the room because the night shift had stayed to help the day shift. Very peculiar to me at the time were the scissors which cut away all my clothes instead of just slipping them off. Obviously, time is of the essence with heart failure.*)

As you can tell, by this time I was very aware of all my surroundings, and I was in serious heart attack trouble. The realization also struck me that Marla's call to my dear wife, Erin, had gotten her off a shift in a surgery unit in a nearby hospital.

At this tense moment, I saw the cardiac monitor, which visually and audibly recorded my heartbeat as it plummeted to a straight line, producing an alarming, steady whirring. It must be emphasized that this was not another sensational out- of-body experience or (after death experience) ADE. I was watching everything with my own eyes and listening with my ears from the operating table. The steady whirring sound was followed by the most terrifying sound of all! One of the ER docs said in a diminished voice, *"We lost him."*

(I would like to have interviewed the staff later about their impressions of all that happened that fateful day when my heart stopped, but that didn't happen.)

Erin's stealth entry must have caused the ER doctors some concern, as she was in her scrubs but not one of the official staff at that hospital. Her rather strange appearance at the time was also accentuated by her placing her hands over my heart. I was able to put my hand over hers in what I thought was a goodbye embrace as I was slipping away. As if that were not enough, during all the shouting and medical devices, the room fell totally silent as the steady beeping of the monitor was replaced by a fixed whirring sound. She was praying in tongues, *glossolalia*, one of the gifts of the Holy Spirit, as recorded in Scripture. "And they were all filled with the Holy Spirit and began to speak in other tongues, as the Spirit gave them utterance" (Acts 2:4).

Fervent prayer over a dead man.

The ministry of Jesus Christ and his apostles included praying over the sick for healing and even over the dead to be brought back to life! At this moment, Erin did not break down into weeping over the medical evidence that she was praying over her dead husband. This was the ultimate action of faith in waiting on God!

Under these circumstances, one would think that panic would be more in order for me at the thought of my death; however, all that occurred was silence, peace, and calm. To this day, twenty years later, I do not know how long the time was that my heart stopped, and Erin can only remember praying over me. There were no flashes of light, sounds, or sweet aromatic scents.

I woke up some time later with Erin as my first sight. I was moved to an intensive care unit with the now too familiar sound of the cardiac monitor proceeding at a reasonably steady pace with no stopping or alarms. I would remain there for five days and then be moved to a Telemetry floor with a *holter monitor* (a mobile EKG) strapped to my chest for monitoring the condition of my heart from another floor in the hospital.

The only comedy in this near tragic part of my story is what happened next. The small electronic device, with at least eight wires taped to various parts of my chest and strapped to my body, had a small, battery-powered red light that was slowly growing dimmer and dimmer until it finally disappeared. By the clock on the wall, it took twenty-five minutes for a nurse to rush into the room and check and see if my heart had actually stopped after it was finally noticed from another floor. I said, "It looks like I died twenty-five minutes ago, and it sure was nice of you to check on my corpse."

After a red face and convincing apology, she replaced the eight new batteries that are supposed to be dependable. All was well for awhile . . . until the same scene was repeated three more times over the course of several days. When I was finally discharged from the hospital, I did thank the staff for my good care with an honest sentiment of gratitude. When relatives, friends, and colleagues asked me about my recent heart attack, I had to confess that I "died" five times: once for real and four more times because of battery troubles.

Getting back to the true story of a *dead man watching*, my survival was and remains to this day a *miracle!* Our relative was a resident in medicine at that time, and Erin sent my hospital records to him for his consultation about what had happened.

The medical record was shared with cardiologists on staff there, and their responses were significantly similar. The consensus was, "There is no way this patient survived the magnitude of this heart attack."

The medical description of my event included an anterior cardiac artery completely blocked, resulting in a myocardial infarct (MI) to 35 percent of my lower heart muscle. The Italian translation reads *morta della* or "dead meat." My medical records show that the bottom of my heart is scar tissue and, according to present-day medical science, will not function again.

Thanks be to God, to this day I have not experienced the typical heart pains under stress (angina) requiring the use of *nitroglycerin* that could become a daily routine for heart attack survivors. I did the research in preparation for seminars to be presented to a system-wide staff of aging teachers. The resulting seminars provided some scary statistics. In 45 percent of all heart attacks, the *first real sign of heart disease* and/or atherosclerosis (plaque in the arteries) is DEATH! Medical science has moved far past my remote northern town experience. Today, more sophisticated methods are available to help with the diagnosis and treatment of coronary arterial diseases.

Needless to say, we remain thankful on an hourly basis for the blessing of a healthy heart life for many years. There was the statistical risk of a second episode within the same year. The actual date of this episode was the winter of 1997, and it has been twenty years without another heart attack.

Another blessing of this story is the fact that after many years there have repeatedly been opportunities to witness to what God has done in my life. One recent event involved a meeting with two Orthodox nuns while shopping in a grocery store. After some pleasantries, I shared some of my story, which begins with the title of this book. After listening intently to my story, they looked at each other, whispered a few words, and agreed that I should change my name! "It should be Lazarus." This scene has been repeated several times in different settings.

It has occasionally been a question in my mind as to what Lazarus would have said about his experience of death. (*I'm sure that he was eager to share his remarkable story with anyone who would listen.*) Unfortunately, little is said about Lazarus after he miraculously walked out of his tomb after being dead for four days. His sister was upset with Jesus for showing up too late and warned Jesus that Lazarus would stink with the corruption of death.

"Lord, by this time there will be an odor for he has been dead four days" (John 11:39).

Because psychological and emotional stress is often identified as a major catalyst for heart disease, I was advised that I should go on a medical leave for some rest and relaxation. We moved to the home we already owned in the south. With family and friends there, it truly was a time to regroup and set a new course. My teachers' pension was moved up without penalty thanks to legal help and support from friends in *Mended Hearts,* a hospital heart recovery group. As a result, we were blessed with an income, which freed us from being concerned about living expenses.

Looking back on how that evolved is another sign of God's mercy in our lives. Too often a medical disaster is combined with the follow-up financial catastrophe. At the time, we had one entering university and one in high school, while the other five were setting out on their own adventures, including missionary work, further schooling, and even professional football. We were very blessed to have an income and the time to deal with all the family's progress and varying needs.

CHAPTER TWO

EXTREME STRESS: THE CAUSE OF MY DEATH?

The back-story to this first heart attack was very closely linked to the impact of stress in one's life. The definition of heart disease can best be understood when read as *dis-ease*. While still teaching at the high school level, I had the opportunity to take a sabbatical leave for the purpose of graduate study abroad. I already had a master's degree, so my lifelong dream was to get a PhD. *What a mistake that would turn out to be.*

The first step was to apply to a university. With the graduate record and entrance exams completed, we were ready to pick up and move the family two thousand miles to the "scene of the crime." All this was done without first investigating the department and the faculty. I have found after many conversations with scholars holding earned doctoral degrees that the case described here is not at all rare.

The first rude awakening to the nightmare was meeting my doctoral counselor. Consider this scene: dressed in a suit and tie, I met a man who looked like a character in a movie about a shabbily dressed hobo. He smelled like a mixture of body odor, cigarette smoke, and alcohol. He was unkempt and had huge bags under his bloodshot eyes. He smoked continuously. This was Dr. Morris Burnt-out. He opened with the confession that his doctorate had cost him his marriage and that he was, in fact, a recovering alcoholic. *It sure looked and smelled like there had been no recovery.* First impressions aside, I focused on the task in this "counseling" session to set up my course of study and classes for the first two semesters. The degree process had commenced, and this was only the first in a series of associations with bizarre faculty members.

The first encounter with my faculty advisor.

One of the strangest of the department mainstays was Dr. Alice Newager. Well-dressed and very smart-looking, with an oversized crystal pendant around her neck, she seemed professional. However, this class of thirty students was immediately on high alert when she spent her introductory class talking about her personal belief system and her spiritual awakening to the wonders of the New Age movement. This all transpired without reference at any time to her curriculum.

Each hour-and-a-half class from then on was spent with the first thirty minutes proselytizing her captured audience about the New Age movement. Two of the most peculiar sessions began with her excited claims of having recently fixed her husband's crashed computer from her office miles away . . . while his computer was turned off. The other was about her New Age guru from a nearby city who flew to Detroit on a mission without the benefit of an airplane. It sounds absurd, and these accounts are not fiction but they tell more about the troublesome conditions in which the doctoral students were ensnared. A popular myth in our culture is that a person with a higher degree from even a prestigious university is not only well-educated but also an ethically sound person.

Another of my strange experiences the next year was with Dr. Marguerite de Sade, whose specialty was calculations. After navigating through four nearly disastrous statistic classes, I renamed the courses "Sadistics." The concluding *Sadistics* 600 "do or die" was required with no alternative instructor.

The first day of class was a real clue about how it would all go for one full semester. She stomped into the classroom. There were twenty-five nurses vying to have "Dr." in front of their names for possible employment in hospital administration, whereas there were only three men working on their respective doctorates. She slammed her briefcase on the desk. The men assumed she was another one of the nurses. Her opening statement was, "I have a reputation on this campus for hating men."

This actually happened. The nurses stared in disbelief at the men in the room. By the second week, one male could not take the gender prejudice any longer and quit the doctoral program. He was at the finish of his course work and he quit! One of the females in the class was not a nurse: Theodora, affectionately known as "Teddy," became a close friend and was a welcome support to the two remaining men.

One class of note was the one when my question

was raised about statistical *outliers* (e.g., an individual sample extremely beyond the norm). The question was whether it was legitimate to remove them from a sample. Some of the nurses gasped and looked at me with shocked expressions. My friend Teddy stared at me in serious disapproval. *(Was there actually smoke coming out of the instructor's ears?)* The weekly investment of twelve hours doing the calculations for one problem became a weekly disaster. My papers were returned with many unkind and discouraging red statements and too often a grade of C!

At the conclusion of the class on the day of the final exam, we all met in a small classroom in a remote building on campus. Dr. de Sade marched in and slammed the exams on the desk, announcing that the exam would "start at eleven a.m. and end at one p.m. sharp." There was, however, an abrupt change to her schedule that was sure to embarrass her in the department. A fire alarm went off at eleven, and we all had to march out to a distant courtyard.

With a visible amount of consternation, Dr. de Sade made a quick phone call to the administration as to what to do for a new and safe room. Who had called in the bomb threat? The list of suspects included the most likely one: the poor man whose doctorate terminated with her class. Was it some of the nurses who were fed up with the instructor's condescending opinion of men? Or was it Teddy, in retaliation for all the grief the instructor had caused to Ben and me? Finally, was it Ben or me? The last three were the only "*not guilty*" answers to the question we could be sure of. After the exam was completed and a good laugh outside, the three of us kidded, "It wasn't me. Was it you?" To this day we don't know who made the threat, and Teddy went to her grave within a few years of her doctorate completion not knowing along with the rest of us. When the class ended, the nurses and Teddy all had A's and the two remaining men had the only B's. A letter grade of C would have meant expulsion from the doctoral degree program.

I completed all my course work, went through the dissertation proposal, and, with significant maneuvering, established a dissertation committee. I did the research, had the dissertation completed, presented and defended without problems.

After the successful completion of the program requirements, the real obstacle started with the department head, Dr. Harold Gelding. He had been at my defense presentation and verbally approved the work; however, this positive affirmation was to radically change. He called me into his office to announce that my document was "not acceptable." When asked what made it so, his answer was presented as a challenge. Either I change my dedication page or the dissertation would not be advanced to the graduate dean for acceptance, publication, and the granting of the degree. His issue was the simple statement that did not include gratitude for him or any member of his department. It simply read:

"THANKS BE TO GOD."

It has become politically correct behavior for academics in modern America to categorize and treat Christians as ignorant, superstitious, and unscientific.

We had to leave for home, as my sabbatical leave, time, and money had run out. The entire family relocated, not knowing the conclusion but trusting that my protests would be honored.

The amazing conclusion was found in the mail. I say it was amazing for two reasons. First, the letter was addressed to:

John Haart, Canada

How it got to my correct address without the necessary number, street, city, and zip code was not the only amazing fact. The contents indicated that my dissertation was a "mess" and that I would have to start all over on a new topic! All this happened after it had been successfully defended without any challenges before the entire graduate school, including Dr. Gelding.

This was a painful disappointment to say the least. That notification from the department head had generated a great deal of disappointment and anger. All seemed finished, but I called an old trial lawyer friend in the same town to explain my dilemma. After hearing that all possible remedies had been exhausted, he proposed to file *An Intent to Litigate* with the state Attorney General against the university for reneging on their duty to grant my earned doctorate.

During the next couple of years, life continued with a lot of prayers, but I was still angry about the injustice of it all. A dramatic breakthrough in the stalemate happened one day at a church we attended. We were greeted by one of the very few people who knew of our situation and who had been praying and fasting on our behalf. He surprised us with a scripture quote. He read the following from his Bible:

"Be still before the Lord and wait patiently for him; fret not yourself over him who prospers in his way, over the man who carries out evil devices. Refrain from anger; forsake wrath! Fret not yourself; it tends only to evil. For the wicked will be cut off; but those who wait for the Lord shall possess the land" *(Psalm 37:7-9).*

A prophetic word of encouragement

Needless to say, the letter from Dr. Gelding had inflicted a great deal of disappointment and I was angry."Be angry but do not sin; do not let the sun go down on your anger"*(Proverbs 4:26).* Further commentary from the same fellow parishioner included, "Trust in God, do not be angered, your tribulation is over. You will seek your former enemies and they will not be found." Erin and I were comforted with this prophetic message. My life was in turmoil and now finally received, this word of consolation.

The next stage was a surprise call to our home from the dean of the graduate school, Dr. Angel Powell. After stopping and holding the phone down while stifling intense emotion, I listened carefully. *Was she calling to explain why my doctoral degree could not be granted?* I stopped breathing.

"John, your dissertation has finally reached my office. I've read your document, and although it's not an area I'm familiar with, I think your dissertation is quite good. So my question of you is, what date do you want us to put on your degree?" After holding down the phone for another pause, through my tears of relief I managed to get out, "Any date you want!"

The large document which authenticated the doctorate arrived later on in the mail. We said goodbye and I could hardly believe what had just happened. It is finished. Praise the Lord! The total cost in dollars of the degree was over $125,000 in lost wages, tuition, and housing. And, as you can now understand and appreciate, the most valuable loss could have been my life!

The final postscript came the following summer when we took time to go back to the same town on vacation. I could go to Dr. Powell's office and thank her in person. Erin came with me as we had been in the battle together all the way. On our way out to the parking lot we went to the office complex where the small department had been for years. *Would Dr. Gelding and the rest of the department of disaster be there?*

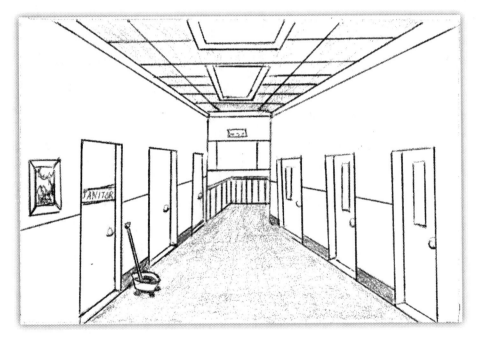

Where have all the faculty gone?

The first office we went to no longer had his department head name plaque. Instead, there was a modest sign that identified the "Janitors." The various other office doors had none of the infamous names of the department members: Dr. Morris Burn-out, Dr. Alice Newager, Dr. Marguerite de Sade, and some others not identified here were all missing.

Upon further inquiry at the school, we were informed by the acting dean that the department had been through "some difficulties," was disbanded, and might be restructured. We left his office without comment in the full knowledge that God had provided the miracle as prophesied by the person at church. "Yet a little while, and the wicked will be no more; you look well at his place, he will not be there" (Psalm 37:10). It was also discovered following the successful completion and publication of my dissertation that six more doctorates from the former department were granted by the university. Following another series of incredible circumstances, my dissertation was expanded into a book that was coauthored by a widely published Christian professor from another department in the same university.

My final word of advice for any and all who think they might want to pursue a PhD is presented here with heartfelt conviction. *Be careful about where you apply and be sure to travel to the university to investigate into what you are about to invest your time, money, and perhaps more. Don't blindly sign up because you succeed in the application process. Once you begin the huge investment, you are trapped with only your good intentions.*

CHAPTER THREE

AFTER THE END

All was well and good for many years after the heart attack and completion of the doctorate: the graduations, the weddings, the grandchildren born and adding to the family number. At the time of the writing of this book, there are twenty-two grandchildren in all. Praise the Lord!

After a few years in Canada, we returned to the USA to spend our golden years in retirement. I received a surprise invitation to the Graduate School of Education in a small Christian college out west. That episode was another strange twist in this story. Erin and I were flown out to interview and meet with college administration and faculty. The process concluded after three intense days of interviews. Keep in mind that it was very clear that I am a Catholic and this was a Protestant university.

When the provost challenged me, along with some others about the Reformation and what I had missed. I simply answered, "Let's not go there."

At the conclusion of three intense days, we found ourselves sitting in a large circle of staff and administration with about fourteen people. After a few more questions, the provost had a pivotal question for me. "After all of our questions of you do you have any questions for us?"

Without hesitation or consulting Erin, I confessed my real response . . . one you should never give at a job interview. Remember, I already had a good income from my pension, so I didn't really need the professorship. I simply said, "You would all make my life much easier if you would not offer me this position on your faculty of education." All conversation ceased. After a sustained period of silence and then some courteous farewells, everyone got up and left the room.

When we exited the door, we both glanced at each other and silently agreed that would be the last we would hear from them, but God had another plan. We left to take a plane back to our home where we received a surprise call from the Dean of Education. To my amazement, she offered full professorship with one year of tenure and the potential for permanent tenure. This was an impressive offer in academia for a new hire. Rather than accept on the phone, I said we would consider their generous offer. We prayed about it and received the answer that I should take the position.

I had recovered from the heart attack trauma and was looking forward to training secondary teachers. So we picked up again and moved to our new home. Those job benefits lasted for four years and provided for Marla's bachelor's degree. Micah finished high school there, and he met Lydia, who would eventually become his lovely wife. Erin and I are convinced that the job had a purpose. "We know that in everything God works for good with those who love him, who are called according to his purpose" *(Romans 8:28)*.

At this time, the largest single group of our family was residing up north. We chose a geographic location close to all three families, and our new residence was established.

In the following years there began a new phase in our retirement living with the purchase of a beautiful, little home in the south with our son, Mark. With winter stays of two to six months per year, we began to lead two lives, each with family, friends and Christian communities. It was a blessing to be able to spend cooler summers up north and warm winters in the southern part of the United States.

PART 2

CHAPTER FOUR

ARE YOU GOING TO TAKE MY LIFE NOW, LORD?

All went well until one early September morning in 2011 in our home. I got out of bed only to collapse on the floor unable to get up. *I know I'm not dead, but why can't I move?* When she heard the thump on the floor above, Erin rushed upstairs to see what happened. Her RN training identified my problem as a stroke: *sudden paralysis/numbness, on one side of the body (mine was the left side, drooping on one side of the face, confusion, trouble speaking, etc.).* An ambulance and paramedics were at our door within minutes.

(With signs of stroke or heart attack, call an ambulance, as time is crucial for treatment. Also, if the exact time of the event can be verified, this will determine whether or not the patient might qualify

for a clot-busting drug, I was ineligible for this intervention.) The US statistics on deaths per year caused by heart attacks and strokes is over 650,000. (www.CDC.gov). This informative website contains many other helpful directions to learn more about cardiovascular health.

We were off for another trip to the ER, where the CT scan of my brain showed a massive *right hemisphere stroke* caused by a total artery blockage. A subsequent MRI revealed two halves of the brain, black on one side and completely white on the other. The stroke was so massive that one half of my brain appeared dead. Our seven married children dropped everything and flew thousands or drove hundreds of miles to be with us--not an easy task with all those grandchildren left behind and with only one parent in charge of the busy lives that required a team effort on a daily basis.

At the time, my brain functions were so wobbly that I just said, "Hello" to each person as though they'd just dropped in from across the street. Our son, Mark, the fireman with paramedic training, stayed the first night at my bedside and found what was later identified as one of the probable causes of my stroke. During the night, I stopped breathing several times. Mark simply used his pro football strength to lift and turn his 220-pound dad over so he could continue breathing. Micah had night number two and panicked when the same thing happened. This time, his desperate call for help produced what I thought was very strange the next morning. I woke up with oxygen tubes in my nose. *Sleep apnea*, a condition caused by a collapsed airway, had forced stress on my heart and arteries. This was a probable cause of the massive stroke. (*For people who snore loudly: be aware, you also could have sleep apnea and need a CPAP: a Constant Pulmonary Airway Pressure device.*)

The staff neurologist at that time spoke privately that he was quite puzzled that I had even survived given the magnitude of the blockage and subsequent brain damage. Mark brought some cutting-edge ideas about onsite stroke reversal, so I was immediately swallowing quantities of what I guessed might be WD-40, the spray lubricant made from fish oil, used for many decades on cars and household jobs.

Swallowing the expensive Norwegian fish oil that Monica immediately bought became part of my recovery. Amazingly, after a lot of prayers to Jesus Christ offered by many and only ten days in the hospital, I returned home in good shape: *walking, talking, and chewing gum all at the same time!* When we left the hospital, I was curious about two of the many people in my ward who were in wheelchairs with withered hands, heads down, and unable to move. Erin quietly informed me in the car ride home that they had both been there for several months following their strokes. Needless to say, I remain very thankful.

The only residual impairments of the stroke were my sense of taste and problems with music-- both *right hemisphere* functions. The sense of taste disorder was discovered with the nurse's first attempt to see if I could swallow successfully. The effects of a stroke can impede the ability to swallow. I was asked to try some vanilla ice cream as the clinical observation proceeded. The only problem on my end was that I knew the taste should be vanilla (*Even as you read this, you can bring to mind its distinct taste*). However, my big surprise was that it seemed like a terrible trick: *Was this really diesel fuel?* The problem now remained, the hospital food was horrible, not because it actually was, but because my brain was mixing up all the signals and providing false information about the taste of the food on the tray. This malady continued after leaving the hospital.

Thanksgiving Day comes in October in Canada, and for many weeks I quietly prayed that my correct sense of taste would return. In the meantime, Erin was insisting that I eat anything that I could. I lost twenty pounds in that time. Prayer continued that normal taste would return for the wonderful, yearly Thanksgiving Day feast. This was the annual event at Monica's house that several of our families enjoyed together. Unknown to all present at the time was the miracle. On this exact day my sense of taste was normal again. The turkey, dressing, mashed potatoes, gravy, and cranberries all tasted wonderful. What a blessing!

What about the musical ability? It had disappeared as the aftermath of the stroke. The day after returning home from the hospital stay, I took out the violin I had played well for decades to see if it could be played. Not only was holding the left hand on the fingerboard hard to do, the actual memory of the tunes had completely evaporated. I tried a simple Brahms's lullaby we can all hum. No deal. I tried to whistle it, thinking it was just the muscles in my left hand and arm. *What a disappointment!* Despite my best efforts, it was not to be done. To this day, I struggle to get a tune out of my violin, and at church I try to sing the hymns with some success.

CHAPTER FIVE

I CAN'T BELIEVE THIS IS HAPPENING AGAIN!

L ife went on with good medical test results for several years with one exception of another medical challenge in the fall of 2015. This time, Erin and I were fixing supper and I could hardly believe what happened next: sudden chest pain that was all too familiar from decades earlier. We took the first precaution (*With signs of a heart attack, it was recommended to chew on an aspirin.*) Again, an ambulance was at our door in a few minutes. (*Remember this: Call 911 for an ambulance!*)

Back in an ER, this time the technology had advanced to cardiac angioplasty. My arterial system was filled with a dye used for imaging to insert a catheter. The cardiac arteries were entered with a stent (a stainless steel mesh implant used to hold a blocked artery open). As I watched the screen and the tool entered the heart area, I heard the doctor's surprised exclamation as my initial prognosis was a large clot in one of my coronary arteries. "There's nothing there!" exclaimed the doctor. My audible response was, "Praise the Lord."

Early the next day, in a perplexed mood, the cardiologist entered my intensive care room. "I almost could not sleep last night thinking about your images, so I rushed in this morning to review them for any error I might have made." Our only other contact with him was when Erin and Monica got onto the same elevator he was riding. He could only say that my case was a total mystery to him, and he had never in all his years as a cardiologist seen a clot "spontaneously" dissolve. Does it sound more like a miracle and not a mystery? Needless to say, I remain thankful for surviving yet again and remain a formerly *dead man watching*.

CHAPTER SIX

BELIEVE IT OR ELSE: ANOTHER END

That was not the end of that episode. After several days at home, I began to have excruciating abdominal pains. They were so intense that it was obvious something was seriously wrong. I had to leave the room when our granddaughter Emma was visiting us to keep from distressing her with all my pain. It was unrelenting pain for hours, worse than both heart attacks, pain that would not stop while I was sitting or lying down. We were off to the ER again.

Bursting in the door with a demand for "morphine," I was told that was not going to happen. After telling me to calm down for a checkup with no painkiller, it was determined that my urinary system had shut down and was careening toward kidney failure, the typical herald of death. Was this a reaction to the dyes that had been used for the cardiac images a week earlier?

A whole new set of problems started to unfold. After draining a huge amount of urine out of my bladder via a Foley catheter, it was determined that an MRI would provide some answers. Once completed, the images indicated a large mass in my bladder. Then the urologist informed us with the bad news about a suspected bladder tumor. A scheduled cystoscopy would happen as an outpatient within days. The procedure includes inserting a camera with light into the bladder from the front. It was all very businesslike.

The next step was to get the results from my personal MD. He opened with the words you never want to hear after a session with a specialist. "John, I wish I had better news for you. The large mass in your bladder was determined by a radiologist and confirmed by the surgeon from its appearance to be cancerous. The typical protocol will have to be surgery to completely remove your bladder and replace it with reconstruction using a section of your intestine." *Oh no! It sounded like I would get to be a urological Frankenstein.* As if that wasn't enough, there was his additional threat that the cancer may have already spread to nearby organs.

We began a campaign of calls to the same urologist for when this "life-saving" surgery could take place. Weeks of calling without answers raised our anxiety levels to desperation. When we finally got an office clerk to give us a possible date, it was months away because of his heavy schedule.

I called my urologist in the US to describe the unfolding disaster as I was already being treated by him. He said what is nearly comical compared to the Canadian program: "Come in this afternoon." That would be rather difficult to accomplish as we were calling from Canada. We bought flight tickets and were there a few days later on Sunday and in his office on Monday.

He discretely indicated, "We need to take a look at this again." He had already received my medical records from the Canadian urologist, indicating the need for surgery as soon as possible. He did not repeat the unwelcome threats about wishing he had better news. We were back in his office for another cystoscopy on Wednesday of the same week. By this time I was very clear about how it all worked. The camera was used again for the look around to confirm the size and location of the large mass in my bladder.

After years of teaching photography in high school and universities, I was curious about his technique. He continued to circle around and look at the same areas several times. At the end of this intense period of anxiety for Erin and me, as we were watching the same screen, we heard the urologist's conclusion. Audibly surprised, he exclaimed, "There's nothing there!" This was the identical phrase used by the cardiologist when he had looked for a clot in my cardiac arteries. What are the chances of the exact same phrase being repeated? Great relief was followed by his unexpected admission. The surgery he had already booked would be cancelled. He had started the process to do what the Canadian urologist had recommended in his notes but did not do. One might be tempted to think that my records were switched, incorrect, or that *Jesus had healed me* yet again on the flight. Our children and friends, Anita and Edwin, along with many others, had prayed fervently for my healing, and we accepted a prophetic word from Anita that this was "just a bump in the road." Well, the "bump" had absolutely *disappeared.* Praise Jesus!

Once again, I had escaped a disaster by God's

mercy. What else can be said? The prescribed surgery in Canada might have been done needlessly and the medical records might have simply read that "no cancer was removed." Erin had worked for many years in a surgical unit and had seen patients return with serious complications, even leading to death, following unsuccessful surgeries. How can I keep from singing and praising God!

For the first few years after the first life-threatening incident, my anxieties were so great that trying to talk about it typically ended in tears. I would get so choked up that all people could do was feel sorry for me, only leaving me far short of my goal, which was to praise and give thanks to God for His mercy and healing in my life.

The writing of this book has taken twenty years to get up the courage to put it all together. You have not been able to see the many times I have had to stop writing for a good cry. I could only start again "in illegible code" because my fingers were once again in the wrong positions on the keyboard.

As of the time of this writing, I remain in God's hands with relatively good health. My urinary system is free of cancer but is still in need of healing, not uncommon for a seventy-one-year-old-man, let alone a previously *dead man watching.*

PART 3

CHAPTER SEVEN

MY LIFE GOES ON IN ENDLESS SONG

A t this stage the question is very appropriate: Why was my life spared, not once, but several times? The major clue is to go back to the question of why did Jesus save Lazarus. His name means *God Helps*. A simple review of that dramatic salvage of a human life can best be explained by his relationships. First of all, he was Jesus's friend and the brother of Martha and Mary. The story involves His arrival too late to save Lazarus; thus, we find Martha lamenting her brother's untimely death. She questions Jesus about why he didn't show up earlier, before Lazarus died. "Lord, if you had been here my brother would not have died" (John 11:21). The answer was to demonstrate the glory of God. "I am the resurrection and the life; though he die, yet shall he live" (John 11: 25). To this day, it has been my realization that the pivotal person in my being a *dead man watching* my own death is Erin.

She was the Martha who prayed to God to spare and revive my life. I honestly believe that had Marla not been able to get Erin to come to the hospital that fateful day to pray over me, I may have been dead and soon buried.

Going back several hundred words is my reference to the amount of time it took for me to get up the courage to actually write this book. The only person who kept insisting for many years that I must write my story is our dear friend in Christ, David. I was so long in getting started because it is a difficult topic.

If you want to completely halt the progress of a conversation in any context even after a church service, a family gathering, with friends or colleagues, just ask this question:

So, what do you think about death?

You will not get a response. People usually do not and will not talk about this taboo subject. When was the last time you talked about death? It's not even a topic on the obvious occasion when it is the reason for a gathering: a ceremony, celebrated or grieved.

You might never hear the word *death* at a funeral. Today's society's code word is "passed." I know it is so obvious that you don't even want to read this brief challenge *so let's drop the subject.*

In my case, I now know that my life has been spared so that I might become what is on the front page of this book: a witness to the mercy and power of God. How was that to happen? The seed was planted with the Charismatic Renewal in the Church and continues to spread world-wide to this day. This includes the gifts and power of the Holy Spirit we heard about from the pulpit, in the media, and from Catholics and many other Christians everywhere.

We were presented with amazing opportunities that began to emerge in Canada and the USA. Remember that Erin and I together now have two lives. The one in Canada has included a hobby retirement job in southern Ontario as a classic car appraiser. It means that to promote my insurance-related business, I drive a rare 1985 Mercedes 500 SL roadster to cruises and shows in the area.

A few years ago I was inspired to change this otherwise materialistic celebration of the valuable cars driven to these shows by aging men in their sixties, seventies, and even eighties. These men are reliving the dreams of their youth. They couldn't afford or get that car back *in the day,* the '55 Chevy Belair convertibles, but now they are retired and have the time and money for their old favorite car. They drive around to show off their prized possession. Does that all sound a little crazy? Well, it really was, and when I finally realized that I was just one of the rest of the old guys bragging about my car, it was time to do something with the gift I had been given. As a grateful and revived dead man, I have the responsibility to witness to God's gift of life. This was the beginning of my journey that can best be called Car Show "going fishing." The first stage of fishing is to bait your hook. In my case, this fishing ministry starts with something to catch the eye of the subject.

Completely unlike any other of the expensive large signs that are displayed at the front of the prized possession cars, my sign changed dramatically. Instead of just bragging about rarity, cubic inches, and horsepower, my sign now concludes with a totally unique statement. This rare car was "driven to this car show by a dead man."

Going Fishing

I am always strategically seated in my lawn chair next to the front fender, watching as admirers of the car stop to read the plaque. Those who get to the bottom are at times visibly surprised to read the most important part of my sign. I see wives elbow their husbands, and then they both look at me puzzled. *There, I got a bite.* A few just read, look at the car and walk away. Usually they ask if this is my car, and if I am the man in the car plaque story. The catch has begun. There it is, my opportunity to talk about the subject that no one ever wants to talk about: death and what happens after death.

The church-going folks that stop are blessed by the testimony of God's mercy as the plaque concludes. Some just ask about what it means. That's when it is time to get to work; it's my clue to ask a pivotal question. "Do you know where you are going next?" Their simple answer is typically, "To look at the rest of the car show." That is followed by the next stage. *No, do you know where you are really going next?* By this stage in my "go fishing" ministry, the typical answer is, "I don't know." There it is: an opportunity to really witness, just as the red-headed girl in New York did.

My answer is a bold confession. "I know where I'm going. Do you want to know where you are going?" By this stage the navigation gets sensitive with a total stranger. It's time to fire off a quick arrow prayer for the Holy Spirit to guide me to the next, and what might be my last, statement. If they say, "How do you know where you are going?" My answer is about God's mercy and my confidence in what the Gospel is all about and clearly contains. "For the word of God is living and active, sharper than any two-edged sword, piercing to the division of soul and spirit, of joints and marrow, and discerning the thoughts and intentions of the heart"(Hebrews 4:12). I have even had the opportunity to pray with people who start to open up a little with stories about dying or dead relatives. The car plaque has worked as an effective bait and hook and this cold call has started the process. Think about it! How many times in the past ten years has someone introduced himself as a "dead man" or asked you if you want to go to heaven or where your final destination might or should be?

This has been all about how my "fishing" ministry typically happens. I don't keep any records but simply expect in faith that many small conversations about God's love have or will at some point in the future have the intended impact. Sometimes I am planting, and sometimes I am harvesting. "The sower sows the word" (Mark 4:14).

Perhaps one of the most difficult cases was the seventy-year-old owner of a rare Cadillac parked near my car. He stooped over and spent an intense period of time reading my plaque. He responded with some indignation. "So, what does this mean? "When I moved through my sequence of questions he had the response I was not prepared for and never hope to hear again. "I'm going to hell!"

Speechless for a moment and after a silent prayer, there was only a whisper, due to the fact that I was so grieved by his abrupt and serious condemnation of himself. The words of an old hymn started to emerge. "Softly and gently, Jesus is calling, come home, come home." Inspired, I entreated him, "Please sir, just pick up the phone." He slowly turned away without response. The biblical story of the rich man and Lazarus (Luke 16:19-31) provides guidance for this situation: "Neither will they be convinced if someone should arise from the dead" (Luke 16:31).

I can only pray that this encounter might cause him to reconsider what must be a desperate interior life without hope. The fishing ministry continues all summer with one or two classic car shows per week.

Leaving for the southern United States each November means the end of the car show ministry and the beginning of the completely different ministry in our American life. We had a great personal blessing there a few years ago when we met a special, dedicated couple from Indiana one Sunday after Mass. Denny and Margaret Ann have been involved in Pro Life action for many decades, so they invited us to their "sidewalk ministry," praying to save little Americans from death by abortion every Tuesday and Thursday for approximately four to five hours each time.

Without this ministry, we might be like many of the snowbirds that enjoy winters in the South at the beach or on the golf course, having fun in the sun. It is a blessing to be involved. We sit on the sidewalk in front of a death camp as real as Auschwitz in the 1940's. We pray for God's mercy for the women in difficult and sometimes desperate situations who have come to have their own children terminated. We have had to call 911 for medical help when a hemorrhaging, botched abortion victim in the back seat of a car was in a life-threatening condition.

Praying for the lives of the babies and their mothers.

Erin is committed to helping moms say *yes to life* for their little ones. Along with several others who are very knowledgeable and prayerful, she is a sidewalk counselor for those in need of support in what is often a challenging and fearful time. Young mothers are provided with information about the lives of the babies within them and given material about medical help and many other avenues of assistance. The counselors stand near the driveway, hand out informative pamphlets, and talk to those who are headed toward the abortion clinic. We keep records of those who come out and say they have changed their minds. Over the past several years, we have averaged a good number of lives saved per winter season.

The pregnancy homes are in some cases a lifesaver. It is not just *"save your baby and go on your way as best you can."* Instead, these are well-functioning residences for young mothers who are commonly abandoned by the fathers, their friends, and family, and with no place to go. The pregnancy outreach in our city provides them, about twelve at a time, with complete housing, a free meal plan, training, education, babysitting, and a clothing allowance. The stay is for three full years. The ministry costs about six thousand dollars per year per mother.

The results are substantial. Some of the new moms are from difficult backgrounds with heartbreaking details. The opportunities at this outreach have provided very good results. One of the moms we met and talked with had completed her GED and gone through nurses' training. That is why we tell friends and acquaintances in both countries that we get to go to *lifesaving* down South. The typical confusion about this description is that others think we are going to swimming classes. That is our opener for invitations to review another form of the *death taboo of abortion* in our society.

Awareness of the abortion industry in Canada and the USA is a topic not to be discussed at any time and particularly at church. Often, people do not want to know what is going on, just like the German public did not want to know what the Hitler régime was doing in Auschwitz, for example.

This whole ministry is not without its challenges. One year the owner of the failing office complex in the low-income area, where the so-called "clinic" dedicated to "women's health" is located, tried to stop us. What about the health and safety of the innocent child that would become another statistic in the death records? What about the physical, emotional, spiritual health and welfare of the woman, who would choose not to respect and protect her own child's life?

The owner had the police come with the attempt to make us get off the public sidewalk. Pro-life activism is not welcome in the society and particularly with the pro-death and gender mixed-up media and politics in North America in recent times. A national legal support team for pro-life people being harassed by organizations dedicated to abortion in America showed up to help. The lawyers argued for us that we were not impeding traffic, as the police had charged, and that we had every legal right to be on the public sidewalk praying and speaking at the corner of the driveway. (It should be noted that the abortion clinic was distantly out of sight from where the counselors were stationed.) The plaintiff was charged a substantial sum in legal fees and court costs as ordered by the judge who had ruled the same way ten years earlier about the same issue. As far as we were concerned, the point was to gain a just decision that had nothing to do with financial gain. Of course, it did not even reach the news in the local area. But, we did win and as a result can continue life-saving!

CHAPTER EIGHT

THE M LIST OF FAMILY MIRACLES

B elieve it or else. There is a family tradition of barely escaping death. Here are a few of our testimonies.

Our oldest daughter, Marina, started out as very athletic and very much of a risk-taker. After her first mission trip with a teen mission outreach, she went to work full-time for that same teen missions outreach. She traveled all around the globe as she worked her way to an executive position that placed her in charge of thousands of teenagers each summer with trips to different countries on every continent.

She had so many stamps in the back of her passport that they had to add extra pages. Their evangelization methods included what are known from the Middle Ages as "mystery plays" in mime, notably the life, death, and resurrection of Jesus Christ. Marina met renowned people like Mother Teresa of Calcutta in India. She also met the converted tribal member who took part in the killing of five missionaries in the jungles of South America. Marina was in an active war zone, dodging bullets and mortars in Nicaragua. She was even mugged on the streets of Morocco.

She narrowly escaped death in the jungles from charging elephants, hippos, and alligators. It sounds like I'm making this up, but I'm not. A most serious threat on her life was in 1988, the year that a nuclear reactor in Chernobyl, Russia, exploded into a meltdown and sent a radioactive cloud over northern Europe. Ironically, she had no idea of the disaster because the Russian government successfully delayed reporting the story in Europe. We encouraged her by phone to leave as soon as possible because of her close proximity to Kiev in the Ukraine, an area which is still experiencing the deadly effects of the nuclear fallout.

Years later she married Jeff, and she and her husband are now raising three children: Annabel, Jake, and Jillian.

Our third daughter, and second on the list of

miracles, is Monica. While working in the US at a large interstate trucking company, we received an emergency call one cool day in January of 1993. It was our dear son-in-law. He and Monica had just married that summer and were living in eastern Canada where he was in graduate school.

The call reported that Monica had been experiencing spells of blindness and extreme migraine headaches. The prognosis after tests and images of her brain was not good. They indicated the cause was a tumor the size of a walnut at her pineal gland in the very center of her head. The neurosurgeon's report was about the very delicate operation that could take as much as ten hours. The results of this brain trauma included the warning for them to be aware of the possible dire consequences of the operation. Monica could come out blind, or deaf, or both. If unsuccessful, the operation could be fatal. Within a few days, we were all in the waiting room praying for the success of the procedure by one of Canada's notable neurosurgeons.

The waiting room had two other families in the same type of life-or-death situation. One was a motorcycle accident victim. His injuries later were to be the cause of his death. The other family had a similar concern about a brain tumor.

Monica's operation included entering her skull from the rear at the base to lift her brain and insert a metal tube about one inch in diameter so the tumor could be extracted with forceps. Thank you, Lord Jesus, the biopsy was negative. What an answer to prayer. Monica survived and made it through well. The daunting procedure included the insertion of a shunt, or drain tube, from the base of her brain down her neck to the top of her stomach to relieve fluid pressure from her cranium and may have remained there to the present.

In the subsequent years since this traumatic episode, Monica and her husband have been blessed with their four children: Lara, Kate, Jonathan, and Emma.

The third and most recent family near-death experience was also close to the dead man watching story and would be our Christmas miracle of 2015.

Melora, our second daughter, had been ill with a terrible flu for several days when her husband found her unresponsive on the bathroom floor. With some difficulty, she was rushed to a local hospital. The prognosis was very bad.

We received her husband's call at our winter home on the Gulf coast about 180 miles south of their suburb in Orlando. We presumed the call was about their plans to come to our house the next day for Christmas and the holiday celebration. The presents were under the tree and all the food was ready. What a shock to hear of Melora's dire situation. We loaded up our van not knowing if we would arrive three hours later for a serious operation or the preparations for a funeral. Her blood pleasure had fallen to a low of fifty over thirty, next to nothing. She had pericardial effusion (e.g., fluid around her heart), inhibiting the heart's ability to pump. All this was happening on Christmas Eve. The difficulty in finding a cardiologist to deal with this life threatening condition was quite serious. The next stage was a plan to send her by helicopter to downtown Orlando for help from a competent specialist. That was delayed until the morning, and she was transported by ambulance to that hospital.

The cardiologist in Orlando Central was forced to do an emergency removal of fluid in the pericardium around her heart. Her heart had nearly stopped. He announced with alarm to Melora, "You're dying!" Sound familiar to "We lost him?" Anyway, he opened her chest to place a drainage tube as quickly as he could to remove the fluid that was seriously restricting her heart function. It wasn't the less invasive procedure that had been originally planned, but it worked. Although barely living, she had survived. She left the hospital five days later in extremely weak condition, weighing only ninety-eight pounds.

We stayed a month to help out with taking care of their three children: Ashley, Andrew, and Emma. All the household chores and school pickups and drop-offs after the Christmas break were reminders for Grandma and Grandpa of how much work, challenge, and joy was involved with having a young family.

Their Christian community was very generous to bring over meal after wonderful meal, including a complete holiday dinner with all the trimmings on Christmas Day. The children only knew that mom was in the hospital without the awareness of the fact that she might never come home again.

For many days and nights, all Melora could do was get out of bed to use the washroom. She was so weak after the medical trauma that recuperation would take several months. Erin stayed to help for another month by herself. She was a full-time RN, kitchen staff, house cleaner and day/night care for the kids. It was a lot of work, but, again, the story included mother Erin's intervention in a critical moment. Like the pivotal entry into the ER of her dying husband in Canada, she was a needed blessing for Melora and their family in Orlando. She returned to our Florida home in late February, and we went back again to lifesaving together.

Melora took a long time and, with a lot of help, made it through the winter. By spring she could walk around her patio in the backyard. She recovered enough to apply for and get accepted to a graduate school program in law late that summer. When starting a family, she had retired from Associate Dean of Arts & Sciences and was well qualified and blessed to get a generous scholarship. This was another lifetime dream that had almost ended in death before it got started.

The fourth family miracle was Mark, *the hero*. We say this because he was in the news for his recognition by the mayor of his city. Mark was the courageous fireman who rescued two people in a burning convertible on his long drive home from our family reunion. At risk of an imminent explosion, he jumped out of the family van at the edge of the city to rip off the top of the convertible and pull out to safety the two crash survivors trapped in the car, which was resting on its side. All this time, the front of the car was in flames and could have exploded at any minute. He would not tell us about this dramatic save, but his dear wife Mary called to give us the news.

That was not the only event that year. He has always been involved in body-building as part of his training through college football and pro ball in the CFL. But this could have all ended in another instant with a bad accident in a gym. Pulling against a lot of weight ended with a near-death accident. Standing and pulling backwards on hundreds of pounds ended when the cable snapped. The force sent him to the floor backwards to land at breakneck speed on his head.

We got his call from the hospital ER, as he went there with serious pains in his neck. The doctor told him he was lucky to even be alive after what should have been a broken neck, possibly resulting in a wheelchair for life. With some physiotherapy, he recovered very well within a few weeks. Mark and Mary continue to raise their four children: Hanna, Angelica, Joel, and Zach.

Marla, our youngest daughter, was part of a youth missionary outreach to India. Before departing, there was a time of preparation in which the young people were confronted with questions relating to their upcoming journey. They were asked, "What would you do if you were asked to touch a leper?" The responses were generally positive and along the lines of willing to do so for Jesus. However, when Marla was asked, she responded, "No way!" as she was repulsed by the thought of touching someone infected with that disease.

With excited anticipation, the mission outreach team finally arrived in Calcutta, India, intent on being witnesses to God's love and hoping to find opportunities to serve others. However, their enthusiasm was abruptly quenched when, at the train station, all of their backpacks, including their money and passports, were stolen in broad daylight. This event caused them to be sequestered in a hotel while the adult leader tried to have the passports reissued and the stolen funds replaced. This took several days of intense effort.

In the meantime, Marla was becoming restless and decided she would venture out to find Mother Teresa's *Home for the Dying.* She set out alone in a dramatically different environment from what she was used to and, after several disheartening wrong turns, she finally reached the Home.

It was here that she offered to help in any way, such as feeding the residents, sweeping, washing floors, etc. A worker led her to a woman reclining on the floor and told her to hold her while washing her wounds with some cloths that were provided. Marla did so, and as she proceeded to cleanse the sores, the worker said, "By the way, this lady has leprosy."

It can be noted that Father Damian, a Catholic priest, had died of this same illness, when over a century ago he ministered and lived among those who suffered with leprosy. Marla, in fact, did not contract the disease, but through this experience and many other notable ones, she concluded, "*I know that God is real!*"

The remaining family miracles include some of our children who have been in auto accidents in one place or another. The list starts with Michelle, number four, now married to Ralph. Their children are Jack, Grace, Luke, and Joy. Marla and Brent have three children: Kaden, Riley, and Wyatt. Micah, number seven, had his memorable car accident when he was fourteen. In some of the cases there were minor injuries but no fatalities.

It is essential that we should make it clear that we are and have been for many decades a family who believes that a ***family who prays together, stays together.*** And we all praise God that He has answered the many prayers offered at both peaceful and frantic times in our lives. "Rejoice always, pray constantly, give thanks in all circumstances; for this is the will of God in Christ Jesus for you" (1 Thessalonians 5:17).

CHAPTER NINE

EPILOGUE

LONG BEFORE THE END

My life began as a child in the northern Ontario town that became the very same place of my death. In fact, I was born in the same hospital in which I later survived death. If that is not enough of a coincidence, I was baptized in the same Italian parish in that very town. After years of suffering through freezing winters, my parents decided it was time to move to better weather in 1946. As a result, the first couple of years were spent in Miami, Florida. Things changed again after one huge hurricane, and it was decided it was time to get out of town. We moved to the other US coast and sunny California. That lasted several years until my dad, the happy wanderer, decided we should move to a dry climate in the Southwest to relieve my mother's asthma. The city we settled in was the very same one I went through grade school and high school and earned my first degree.

All was well for my first six years of life until one night when I woke up screaming with pain in my legs. In a panic, my mother did the only thing she could think of. She wrapped my legs with warm towels and then massaged them with much effort. I discovered shortly afterwards that I could barely stand and brace myself with a chair to get to our bathroom. I don't remember going to a doctor, but I guess my mother had been advised that her original method for relieving my pain was the best and, in fact, the same one that Sister Kenney had pioneered twenty years before in Australia. I had contracted polio. This is the disease that was blamed on public swimming pools and its water-borne bacteria that was common throughout the USA and Canada. Dr. Jonas Salk developed his Nobel Prize winning vaccine in the 1960s.

President Franklin Delano Roosevelt was too late for that treatment and spent most of his adult life with steel braces on his legs and in a wheelchair during his three terms as president. In my case, the disease, which had killed thousands and crippled many more throughout the world, did not have the same devastating effect on me.

After a time of recuperation over a period of months, I did not know why I could not attend school or the secret of why I had to use crutches to get around. I am now left with the revelation that God started to redirect my life at a very early age. He continues to do so, hour by hour. My life goes on in endless song. How can I keep from praising?

When we first started working in that parish in northwestern Ontario, we learned about Fr. Carlo's Scalabrini Order. They are a group of Italian Priests whose ministry in the new world in the nineteenth century was to immigrant Italians in North and South America. Their twentieth century mandate has expanded to all immigrants to the New World. We were very inspired by the founding Bishop's mandate to the order of priests: "Even if all you do in your entire life as a priest is to save one person from hell, your ministry is worth your calling."

This is the point in the book for your piccolo Italiano lesson. Consider the words of an old Italian saying: "ieri, oggi, domani." What does, yesterday, today, tomorrow have to do with the whole theme of this book? As a survivor of polio, two heart attacks, a massive stroke, and a diagnosis of bladder cancer,

I could be living in constant fear and depression. Fear that *yesterday's* medical record could revisit at any moment because of clogged arteries and an unpredictable internal organs. Fear that *today* would be my final day of life. Or fear of the *future* that death would come at an unwelcome time.

However, my trust is in Jesus Christ, who is the same "yesterday, today and forever" (Hebrews 13:8). He is as near as the mention of His Name. He is the Savior, the Healer, the Deliverer, the Provider. He is all we need. His promise is eternal life to all who turn away from wrongdoing, turn to Him for forgiveness, and trust wholly in Him. His "perfect love casts out fear" (1 John 4:18).

> *"Death is swallowed up in victory.*
> *O death, where is thy victory?*
> *O death, where is thy sting?"*
> *(1 Corinthians. 1:.55)*

My life goes on in endless song.
How can I keep from praising?

We trust that these many stories of how God's mercy has worked in our family might inspire the reader of this little book to consider that God is also calling you to trust in Him and accept His wondrous love.

Finally, the end of our witness is found in the very last words of the Bible.

> "Behold I stand at the door and knock; if anyone hears my voice and opens the door, I will come into him and eat with him, and he with me." (Revelation 3:20)

The End

CHAPTER TEN

AT THE LAST MOMENT

At the last moment before publication there was a surprising development in my medical history.

As a requirement of the prostate surgery of early 2017, a cardiologist was needed to verify that my damaged heart could endure the heavy sedation from the anesthesia required for the two to three hour procedure. After some preliminary testing and confirming that it would be safe to proceed, the cardiologist also ordered an echocardiogram to review my heart condition post- surgery.

The first heart attack survival twenty years ago concluded with my survival and the medical prognosis that 35 percent of my heart muscle was dead from the MI (myocardial infarct), and that my heart would for the rest of my life be working with the remaining 65 percent of the good tissue. My EF (ejection fraction) or the amount of actual pumping capacity was identified as "38 percent" which is below normal.

Following the recent test, the conversation with the cardiologist indicated that my numbers had undergone some significant changes. The amount of MI was identified as 10 percent with 90 percent working muscle! My EF was estimated at 55 percent, or within normal limits. These are not changes that ever typically happen according to medical science. In fact, the typical trend is for these two indicators of cardiac damage to remain constant or deteriorate with any subsequent events or simply the passing of time (i.e., getting old).

God has done it all again. This time we got an answer to a prayer that was not on our daily list. My heart condition and function has returned to what it probably was twenty years ago prior to my first massive heart attack and ER flat line episode. The cardiologist's complicated medical record of 4 pages of detailed numbers and ranges could have been included but the entire document can be reduced to: Normal, Normal . . . . Normal.

I continue to pray in thanksgiving:

**"Bless the Lord, O my soul; and
all that is within me,
bless his holy name" (Psalm 103:1).**

**"O give thanks to the Lord, for he is good;
for his steadfast love endures forever"
(Psalm 107:1).**

Printed in the United States
By Bookmasters